Valentines

BY ROD McKUEN

BOOKS

Poetry

And Autumn Came
Stanyan Street & Other
   Sorrows
Listen to the Warm
Lonesome Cities
In Someone's Shadow
Caught in the Quiet
Fields of Wonder
And to Each Season
Come to Me in Silence
Moment to Moment
Celebrations of the Heart
Beyond the Boardwalk
The Sea Around Me
Coming Close to the Earth
We Touch the Sky
The Power Bright & Shining
The Beautiful Strangers
The Sound of Solitude
Suspension Bridge
Valentines

Collected Poems

Twelve Years of Christmas
A Man Alone
With Love
The Carols of Christmas
Seasons in the Sun

Alone
The Rod McKuen Omnibus
Hand in Hand
Love's Been Good to Me
Looking for a Friend
Too Many Midnights
Watch for the Wind

Prose

Finding My Father

Et Cetera

A Book of Days
A Book of Days, 2
Another Beautiful Day
Another Beautiful Day, 2

Music Collections

New Carols for Christmas
The McKuen/Sinatra
   Songbook
New Ballads
At Carnegie Hall
28 Greatest Hits
Through European
   Windows
The Songs of Rod McKuen,
   1
The Songs of Rod McKuen,
   2

MUSIC

Concertos
For Piano & Orchestra
For Cello & Orchestra
For Guitar & Orchestra
#2 for Piano & Orchestra
For Four Harpsichords
Seascapes for Piano
The Woodwinds

Symphonies,
Symphonic Suites, etc.
Symphony No. 1
Ballad of Distances
The City
Piano & String Suites
Adagio for Harp & Strings
Rigadoon for Orchestra
Pastures Green/Pavements
  Gray
Symphony No. 4

Chamber
Piano Trios
Piano Quartets
Sonata for Ondes Martenot

Ballet
Americana, R.F.D.

Point/Counterpoint
Elizabethan Dances
The Minotaur (Man to
  Himself)
Volga Song
Full Circle
The Plains of My Country
The Man Who Tracked the
  Stars
Birch Trees
Liberty
I'm Not Afraid (with
  Jacques Brel)
Seven Cynical Songs

Major Film Scores
The Prime of Miss Jean
  Brodie
A Boy Named Charlie
  Brown
Joanna
The Unknown War
Scandalous John
The Borrowers
Lisa Bright & Dark
Emily
Travels with Charley
The Beach
Imaginary Landscapes

HARPER & ROW, PUBLISHERS, New York
Cambridge, Philadelphia, San Francisco, London
Mexico City, São Paulo, Singapore, Sydney

CHEVAL BOOKS, Los Angeles
Sydney, Amsterdam

Rod McKuen

Valentines

with decorations by the author

FOR CHEN SAM

"I've never written, though I thought I wrote,
never loved, though I thought I loved,
never done anything but wait outside
the closed door."

—Marguerite Duras, *The Lover*

FIRST EDITION

Designed by Ruth Bornschlegel

Library of Congress Cataloging-in-Publication Data
McKuen, Rod.
     Valentines.

     Includes index.
     1. Love poetry, American. I. Title.
PS3525.A264V3   1986   811'.54   85–42578
ISBN 0–06–015501–9

86 87 88 89 90 HC 10 9 8 7 6 5 4 3 2 1

Contents

Author's Note

Valentines make me think of unexpected letters, messages bent in fortune cookies, notes in bottles set adrift, help from strangers in strange towns. Kindness without expectation, the anonymous gift, the unplanned moment (as opposed to those of Grand Design).

Most of these valentines are not lacy-edged, nor do they smell of lavender. Some are small scenarios in search of larger room. A few are jottings that seem to fit all right. There are elegies, a quatrain, and some sonnets. One long section contains sketches of *vox populi* and silhouettes of friends. A few poems range back across an oeuvre that's over. They are here again because they asked to be included. Many more are new. In short, this is a batch of valentines, where love is not so much the subject as is life and death.

The section entitled *Sonnets from the Japanese* has no Asian significance beyond the fact that these poems were completed in Osaka, Tokyo, and Taipei during the second and third weeks of October 1985.

Finally, I am grateful for and wish to acknowledge the extra time and patience my editors Larry Ashmead and Margaret Wimberger gave me, even after the so-called *final* galley proofs of this book were in. Their flexibility as far as deadlines were concerned enabled me to come a little closer to arriving at the book I intended this to be. And, as always, Wade Alexander was on the other end of overseas telephones and overnight mail, dictionary in hand. Nothing works without friends, and you as reader join the circle.

ROD McKUEN

October 22, 1985
Hong Kong

FOOLISH HEART

Correspondence

Endorsement

I love your glances meeting mine
across forever or the room,
your touch is strong enough for me
to hang my aspirations on.
When we hold on to one the other
stars could fall, kingdoms tumble,
dust would never settle on us.

I love your name attached to mine
or stationary on the door,
it gives me new importance.
It's pleasure to be gone from you
because the road leads ever home.
I love your glances meeting mine
across forever or the room.

Valentines

Sentiment comes so easily
some of it must be real,
                heartfelt.
Much of it might be selfish too,
but whoever said a rose existed
                just for the cutting,
not for the pleasure of branch and bush,
and why is an explanation always
needed as amplification for tears?

The heart ages faster than artery, limb,
so why should a lacy valentine be
thought of as whim not thought
                in practice—
and why must words
be willing accomplice to hand on shoulder
                        in grief?

We all know time
        to be the meanest thief,
so why can't sentiment ease its passage,
or what are valentines for?

The Eyes Have It

It's only the rope
finally uncoiling,
the glacier melting at last.
It's only the wind
licking its fingers.
The bird in silent prayer.
The mudlark down
by the river's edge
helping to build the farm.

Only the boatman
crossing the river,
passengers arriving
at The Isle of the Dead.
The derelict hanging out
at the station
thinking God lives
in package stores,
grocery shops.

It's only the boy
who promised forever
losing you in his
soft blue eyes.
Only the dustman
emptying cans.
A little band
at the corner playing
beautiful, difficult lullabies.

Only the miracle
you always prayed for
but certainly didn't expect.
It's only the lovers
down in the park
giving their summer performance.
Only the girl
with blood-stained eyes
saying the song is over.

It's only the roadway
still unpaved
with holes the size
of empty pockets.
Only the locket
you lost or pawned
with nobody's picture
still inside of it
struggling to get free.

Only the spout
of the teakettle whistling,
holding the cup
and saucer hostage.
It's only the cat's eye
fixed on a hen
with spangled plumage,
a red hat on
and no party to attend.

It's only the artichoke
peeled by experts
dropped in the gutter
and sailing beyond
the neighborhood corner,
the edge of the world.
It's only the sound
of the head exploding.

It's only erosion
having its way,
invisible algae eating the sea,
having The State
for bed and breakfast.
Only the melon
being recalled
back to Detroit for repairs.
Nothing but Armageddon.

It's only the shadows
turning to substance
as darkness shudders
and closes its hand.
The eye of the hurricane blackened.
Only the beast
you keep in the basement
coming topside for air.

A messenger only
coming from heaven
to shore up our dreams
and take us away.
Speak in a softer language.
Smile without showing your tongue.
It's only me
on a Thursday evening
coming to you
with a bright smile on.

Nobody's Heart

FOR JULIE HARRIS

I am the blade
that slices the rose
from off of its stem
        to the bottle.

I am the table
the chair is tucked under.
I am the engine's throttle.

I am the willow
with branch downcast
who never looks up
        at the sparrow.

I am the arrow
aimed at the jugular
that enters the heart of the heart.

I am the woman
who sat by the sea
and swallowed the world
            as she waited.

I am the rock
who hit the king's eye
the first week in October.

I am justice,
a little one-sided,
ashamed to be part
            of the system.

I am the name
that wasn't crossed off
pleased to have been invited.

I am the noun
that wants to be useful.
Why am I not a verb?

I am the valentine
still unopened
that nobody ever sent.

I am the opening
you come through
to get to the other side.

I am the valentine
still unopened
that nobody's heart will ride.

For S.C.

I do not know
what is more beautiful
than your tangled black hair
on a white pillow.
I have thought about it all afternoon
and decided not even butterflies or children
or the blossoms in the hills above the beach
can compare.

If I had money
I would not buy a comb or a red ribbon
to decorate it.

Instead I might charter worlds
so you could walk in them
and everyone could see your hair.

Lido Beach

There were no seagulls here today;
warm winds have blown them
off to warmer sands,
to Spain or Greece where there are rocks
and all the caves are
plentiful with clams.

Lying by the sea I watch the *giogoli*
track the ladies down the beach
thinking all the while
of Muir Woods redwood trees,
green fields and sheep dogs,
red poppies seen from train windows.

You wouldn't like the beach today—
the flags are all so tattered,
the kites are all too few.

You'd be like me,
wondering how I came to be here,
not troubled but not happy.

God, I hate this waste of time.
I should be chopping wood
or raking leaves
or home in bed
with all those tired dreams
I saved so carefully
for just such days as these.

I could count the ceiling cracks
and feed the animals
their Crackerjacks.

Though I feel spent,
done out and done,
trying to slow down is not easy
when your thoughts still
hang on yesterday.

Dodging pigeons in the square
while five-piece combos
grate my ears,
I'm restless all day long.

Apart I am
and much alone.

Did you feel the same
while riding home to California?
What were your thoughts and
secret wishes?

I'll tell you this—
you've earned the right to rest awhile
and occupy your time
with just the breakfast dishes.

I know what's happening to us
and I know why.
Outside myself I stand
looking back not in amazement
or in sadness even.
I prop myself against a wall
              in wonder only.

Letter from Sydney

The letter finally came,
bushtail possum
        on the postage stamp,
seven days from Sydney
                to L.A.

No, six,
moving past the dateline
it arrived this morning.

I would that I
were traveling back
with your letter's answer
carried on my tongue
            to yours.

I would look at you
in the easy winter night
of New South Wales
and you would know
that my urgency for answers
to the unframed question
comes from the necessity
of being with you,
not just the luxury of need
to satisfy its need.

You are a fact for me,
        not dream or fiction.

I agree that time
will test us
but time not spent with you
                is lost.

Seattle

I'd like to be a lumberjack again
straddling high trees
    instead of high-born women,
climbing heavenward among the branches
out of the well of meaningless words
I've fallen into from too much city living.

Trees are monuments to God,
        cities monuments to man.
I need to meet my God again
among the ferns and trees.
There's too much *me* in my life now
and not enough of *Him*.

And so I'd like to be a lumberjack again.

Berkeley Hotel

1.
The anemones wilting on the mantelpiece,
the bitter brigade of umbrellas
marching past the window,
queuing down the corner for the bus,
and me without a sleeping pill
          waiting for what?
The rain to stop?
Inspiration to begin?
London to be kind to me?

I do not think Godot will come tonight.
But all the same I leave the window open.

2.
I went back to look for you.
Not understanding the language of hello,
I thought I'd speak it just the same.

I bathed,
left the window open
and one light on.
The heat was off
and as we warmed each other
I knew that you'd make up
for all those dark indifferent backs
that turned from me these many months.

The room sat waiting,
premeditated as a concierge's smile.

In the lobby
there were some roses on a table.
I looked at them so long
I thought the buds had drained
the color from my face.
Finally I went up the stairs
                    to bed alone.

A little drama, unobserved.

3.
I've drawn your face
on tablecloths across the country,
tracing your smile
with my index finger,
making your hair just so,
till now you must be more
what I want you to be
than what you are.

I can paint your eyes and say
this is where I lived
for twenty minutes and some more.

I order grapefruit
and pay for ruined napkins.
And between the morning and the evening
I draw your face a little fainter every day.

Quatrain

If I could have my first life back
I'd treat it better, oh, I would.
I'd tend its ills and feed it good
and guard it from attack.

If not a whole life, half perhaps.
I've much to make up for and I
would take half-life where no birds fly
and women fold their legs to laps.

Not one quarter will you give
to one who wasted life away.
Why are young men taught to pray
if there's no second life to live?

Saturday Night

To see them dance
is such a marvel
whether they run down
the length of Strauss
or stand in place for Stoney End.

Their motions are as fluid
as a kind of liquid neon,
even on a floor so crowded
that each of them appears
to be the other's
next of kin.

The dancing
like the darkness
has no starting place
and seemingly no real end.

If you come here
three nights running
you begin to feel
the night starts only
with your own arrival
and stops as quickly
when you go.

I wasn't dancing
but I wasn't standing still.
I wasn't hunting, but I hoped.
New Year's Eve did not fill up
the forefront of my mind.
I needed not forever,
                    only now.

Maybe I stayed longer
          than I'd planned,
for with the music
and the lateness of the hour
before I'd finished living now
I was driving through tomorrow.

Later on the street
the last fall leaves
were flying through
                    the railings
to float
      along
          the dark
                canal.

Another evening maybe:
with the winter dead ahead
I had three dozen nights
lined up and waiting,
no different from the one
I'd just come through.

I could be content
to walk back slowly
and finally slide down into
that same safe security
that only hotel beds afford.

Knowing that it waited
empty in the darkness,
my footsteps quickened.

I wonder that
no street musician played
The Third Man Theme
for I was surely copycat
or twin to Harry Lime.

Semantics

The difference between
descent and decay
is one has a chance
        of returning.

The obvious over-
looks the next fire
in favor of ones
        now burning.

The pessimist knows
very little at all,
only *I'm tired*
        of learning.

The lover remembers
the good times only
except when recalling
            the bad.

The dreamer extends
the darkness the privilege
of watching his soul
            go mad.

The lover forgets
what he didn't have,
but never the things
            he had.

You can point out mold
                    to some,
bring old diggings
and old bones into a conversation
or show them black-garbed women
who only live to dress the saints,
and they will still believe
that death will never touch them.

These people are protected
by a kind of faith
religion or the mystic
                    cannot follow.
Not just fear but fantasy
is their imaginations' icon.
It is this little band
                    of self-believers
who do great damage, cause distress
and puncture others' lives.

Alas, there are no strangers
                        anymore
and no strange places
                        left to see.
Even Eden has been settled.
And Lazarus could not afford
the real estate to rise from.
The phoenix coming up
from ancient ash and embers
would have to grope his way
through layers of decaying birds.

Hush, hush, don't fret
but be prepared
to go this time and stay.

Baggage

The year was only
one long noisy day
that never knew a quiet night.
                    Your grin
(once strong as any shoulder),
disappearing in so many crowded rooms
each time I thought I'd found your face again,
hardly helped at all.

I suppose it was a glad adventure
                    however quickly gone.
Still, leave me your address
so I won't have to stand in line
                    at American Express.

Thirty-Seven

You may puzzle at me
when I tell you
that your not loving me
is the most love
I have ever had.

But anyone who's
given in to loving
will know and understand.

THE HEART IS A LONELY HUNTER

A Gallery

Irene

She always planned
to go to him but didn't.
Now it would always be too late.
Still she bought roses, lilies,
whatever was abloom
                and perfect,
twice a week and brought them home,
arranged them on the table in the hall.
He would come to her.
The roses would dress up
                an ordinary table.

Looking in a mirror
it was always her aloneness
that looked back at her
so all the looking glasses now were draped.
At night she knelt to needlepoint.
Like some eccentric Joan of Arc
                long past her prime
she dreamed of scythe, not sword.

Dennis

He wears his heart
so skillfully upon his sleeve
most think it just another pocket.
Only Fred Astaire
could dance through life more easily.
If Dante came to visit
he'd ask him if the room
was warm enough
(that's how much he wants to please).

First he fell in love
with faces in slick magazines.
Later on he moved to billboards,
then long commercials in between
small portions of the nightly news.

Beneath the most enormous moon
October ever manufactured
he found, met, fell in love with
                        and brought home
the girl he would have always
                        dreamed about
if he'd known that she existed.
They started to watch TV.
She fell in love with Dan Rather.

Mrs. Allen

She leaves them.
Old gentlemen, old ladies
sharing their pension lunches
             with park birds.
It has started to rain;
her sleep dissolves to widowhood.
Winter will be difficult
but not impossible, unless . . .

Another cobweb
where there was lace before.
Another doily made of dust.
Another rusty teakettle
             to be handled delicately.

Mr. Thomas

He hated the young
because they lived in sleeping bags,
erasing one another and then
prancing into dinner late.
Was it better to wear his hairsuits
than their sweatshirts?

He hated the middle-aged
because after finally shaking off
their fathers' and grandfathers' sins
they still were left with their own mistakes.
But wasn't there room for parity
if not charity, then understanding?

He hated the aged, getting on
because they had no place to go
but back to the damp, the dark
that all of us long ago came from.
Better get used to the dark again,
or have you come up with a better plan?

Maria Louisa

He always said *I love you*
               after every meal.
Sometimes in-between as well.
They'd be waiting in the street,
taking the air, however it was,
and for no reason
out of him would pop *I love you.*
Just like that, the way consumptives
offer up involuntary coughs.
I love you, followed by long silence.
It might have been the hiccoughs
               but it wasn't.

I love you, after shopping.
I love you, after sex.
And when he came no more
               to see her
she was left to wonder
was it love or Memorex?

Emile

He listens to Mahler.
The loneliness grows more monstrous still.
The cat (who has been playing
                          with a ball of hope)
ignores him
and walks into another room.

The telephone rings.
Only silence on the line,
not even breathing or an echo.
Rhythm will ensnare you,
                          he remembers.
A moth eclipses the table lamp.

He undresses carefully.
Sliding his pants down past his knees
he begins to play with himself,
                  then loses interest.
The ache is now between his belly and his head.

And in his head
a bus goes by
belching smoke and stars
is swallowed by a bigger bus
                          blocks away.
He opens his eyes.
Gustav has taken off his hat.

Krystyna

She went back to apple trees
and life beyond the midnight hour,
to rows of predictable houses
on the roads to predictable towns,
to friendly girls of her own age
and all their collective giggles,
to young men courting
                    and the radio,
to mama and brothers and sisters—
home to the Poland
                    she cared about,
away from the California traffic.
Home to 1985 Warsaw
where she would once again know freedom.

Yes, she knew that Solidarity
had been tied and kicked
                    to death;
she heard about it in America
while cleaning a house in Beverly Hills.
But that was somebody else's Poland
                    and anyway home is home
and she went back to be free.
You can't have freedom so far away
where nobody speaks your language
or writes your name down right,
where always, wherever you work,
the dust is inventoried by Madame
three or four steps behind you.

Freedom's the bed you sleep in best,
the pillow you fluff for your own head.
And sorrow's not sorrow when it's shared,
only when done in the dark alone.
And so Krystyna went home.

Eugene Ormandy (1900–1985)

Imagine if you will
Rachmaninoff amid Symphonic Dances
changing partners without thinking,
Mahler, 47, meeting Sibelius, 41,
beyond some unimportant Finland forest.

Mahler: *The symphony must be*
likened to the world. Embracing everything.

Sibelius: *I am not literary.*
The germ and fertilization
of my symphonies are music—
musical only.
The intellectual
confronts the man of intellect
and neither leaves the meeting changed
but everything changes.

The core of art
is what is left unsaid.
No worthwhile dream
comes round full circle
to a certain end.
Here is where the woodwinds enter
                    (and here is where
the strings begin descending).

Give each measure its full measure,
then erase the pencil jottings
            and begin again.

Giants may not track
through these same stalls again
but it's enough to know they came.
That *here* is where they've been.

Jacques Brel (1929–1978)

Reason is
the shortest road to freedom.
Poets know that,
even in the midst of dreaming
or trying out our songs upon ourselves.

And poets always go in quest of freedom
                                    for every man
whose mind has been too long in chains.

I learned the worth of freedom
from your mutterings and frowns;
even now I see you
looking up from some newspaper
to read aloud today's injustice,
pausing on the peaks of paragraphs
to wonder how the world
or one man anywhere
can offer cruelty for lack of courage.

Love is
the only easy way through life.
And who'd have thought
that such an easy road
is paved, repaved and used so often.

The *chansonnier* will tell you
which road is the sure one,
and he's dependable as guide and go-for,
because he wants to get there too.

I learned the worth of love
from all the many ways you said it.
             Pound for pound
more ways of loving came from you
than all the hate most men amass
throughout their lifetimes.

You left behind so many primers
                          on the subject
that generations coming up,
then moving to oblivion,
will find life's starting place
             with greater ease.

But there are far too many mysteries
you made away with,
mornings you took with you,
that none but you will know.

I envy all those unlearned couplets
you hadn't yet set down,
instructions to the world
and even some to me.

Now only JoJo hears your laugh
and shares again your private language.

If only I'd have been there
              for that final minute,
I could have, would have said
              Ne me quitte pas.

Cowboys, One

Brave
they straddle the animals,
hearts racing before the pistol sings,
then leaping from the chute,
man and animal as one,
wedded groin to back.

One small moment in the air
and then the mud.

Hats retrieved,
Levis dusted,
back to the bull pen
to wait the next event.
Sunday's choirboys
in cowboy hats.

Cowboys, Two

Huddled in the pits
below the grandstand
or lining at the telephone
to call home victories
they make a gentle picture.
Their billfolds bulging just enough
to make another entrance fee.

Next week Omaha or Dallas.
San Antonio is yet to come.
And now the Cheyenne autumn
    like a golden thread
ties them till the weekend's done.

Cowboys, Three

They wade through beer cans
piled ankle high in gutters—
the rodeo has moved
    down from the fairground
to the town
and every hotel door's ajar.
Better than the Mardi Gras.
The nights are longer than Alaska now
until the main event begins
    another afternoon.

But after all, the Main Event is still to be
a cowboy
for ten minutes or ten years, it's all the same.
You don't forget the Levis
    hugging you all day
and Stetson hats checked in passing windows
    cocked a certain way.

Some years later
when the bellies
flow over the belt loops
there's always mental photographs.
Here the hero in midair.
Now the Dallas hotel room.
Now again the gaping tourists
licking off the Levis with their eyes.
Photographs of feeling
       mirrored in the mind.

For Bimby

Some things you cannot put down in a new way—
sheep grazing on the airport road from Rome,
stale February days and Bimby's smile.

Balloons never look like clouds to me
                    or Crackerjack surprises
          or anything but just balloons.
So it is with Bimby's smile, held in the Roman day
ablaze with waking tourists and sleeping cats
and ruins being ruined by the tick of time.

Her smile is just her own without elaboration,
lost in the Alitalia afternoon.

David

David in the driveway leaving,
pausing for a moment
but a moment only
and down the driveway gone.

See the night sky, David,
free of clouds at last.
Stars there are and crickets
                    in the trees.
All have moon-blue shadows.
Too many comets uncollected,
enough to fill a hundred
                    Mason jars
and still spill out and over.

Trevor

He keeps a night book
on the table by his bed.
Should inspiration overtake him
in the midnight he's prepared.
Sometimes under the influence
of scotch and water and
sometimes under the influence
of sleeping pills and some
times under the influence
of scotch and sleeping pills
he writes things into it.
But he almost never reads
the notes he jotted down
the night before. Not
because they are irrelevant,
but because the Dexedrine
he takes when he awakens
puts him on a high that
discourages anything that might
have had its genesis under
the influence of artificial stimulants.

Betty and Phil

He was always saying he'd leave
if she continued to wear him down
with word after word of complaint.
Time after time after time
                 and so on.
She would always threaten to go
if he didn't change a few of his habits,
like leaving the toilet seat perpendicular,
the cat locked out, the dog locked in,
and playing Tammy Wynette recordings
ad negative over and over again.

It's a wonder the cat didn't pack
                 its bags,
the dog didn't run away,
the seat of the toilet drop
                 from exhaustion
just from being shouted about.

It must have occurred to them
                        both at once
that some kind of marriage
                        (or other crime)
would have to be committed before
divorce could even be talked about.

Just such details stop many a couple
from becoming unstuck properly.

Fiore/1812

If I could set down eighteen lines
upon a clean white page
that so expressed you
detailed in minute and grand detail,
the sockets of your eyes,
the girth of you
omitting not one millennium
                    of your size,
if I could tell exactly what it's like
to climb through you and into myself
then back inside/outside you again,
or say face to face
in rhyme or out of rhythm
how I feel this day
after only one night's reading of you,
say it straight for your ears only
yet with no complexity
so that everyone would understand,
then I could write my final poem and be done.

I could turn the page
and find a single line that summed it up,
here it is, I'd say, all for you.
Everything I've made from my life
and with my life:
here it is—all I've done
down nearly forty years
from crying in the cradle
to sobbing in the spotlight,
every laugh and long sigh in between
was preparation for just now.

Could I say it well enough
to be believed by you,
I'd run home to Pine Street
and open all the windows
                    W I D E
and shout to all the neighbors,
look who's living here inside—
                    we are
surrounded by a greener green
than any meadow ever knew
and a multi-colored bed
wide as any known or unknown sea.

Fiore! I would shout aloud,
flower of a different hue.
Fiore with a mind of so many unseen colors
that the dahlia or the tie-dyed rose
would never dare compete with you.

If I could set down eighteen lines
on the virgin page
followed by a second twelve
to sum a statement of us up,
I'd dwell on every possibility
leaving out the humps and hurdles.
No impossibilities exist
to keep from bringing each of us
into the realm of one.

Come into me
as I've lately come inside of you.
A fusion we are, best of both
that splits to thirds when we're together.

Now we've come to final spring,
nineteen hundred eighty-five,
and most goodbyes remain unsaid—
                    only hinted at.
Fare well or better
there than here.
If you can use me
            call my name.
It's just the two of us again
on either side of searing flame.

Andy

I saw him in the cowshed
milking metaphors until
no cream came up to settle
        at the top.
The morning chores behind him,
             he took ease
halfway up a haystack.
There no needle found him,
and no farmer's wife with open apron
came to seek out just the right man
        for odd jobs round the house.

It's tough on poets when the muse
decides to take an ocean cruise.
Hard when old analogies are all there is.
A sentence is a sentence then,
not commuted but not carried out.

Halfway up or halfway down a haystack
the poet's dream is empty.
Now cows trail home with bulging udders
        expecting new relief.

Hale Matthews

Finally clear of the treacherous air,
he meets archangel face to face
demanding the peace he did not find
                     in life,
something hinted at
as life was moving from him.
He knows serenity is not
               the only state of grace
and yet it is the only place
where shadows do not haunt
               but complement.
No more darkness, incandescence
          his only wish.
Put me to use by letting me sleep.
Give my speech to someone else.
Someone down there needing help.

Cloud be my protectress
now that the wind has stripped me bare.
I need only a little air.

Greeting those who went before him
he hands out leis of beatitudes,
is mindful of old enemies
                coming on as friends.

So this is the way it happens,
all things rectified, all ends tied up.
If only he'd known this
                in his darkest nights—
that life was only a passing over
                                into life
instead of a silent prayer on airplanes,
the awful crawl toward religion,
life not life except in fleeting.

LIGHT-HEARTED

Sonnets
from
the
Japanese

Railroad Ties

If I had empty pockets still
and empty headed dreams again
the codicil for my new will
would be a ticket on a train.
Trains that tremble through the night
to places only brakemen know,
a train whose rows and rows of light
still brighten up a town ago.

Listen, it's the two-ten coming
same old whistle, note for note,
rails and telegraph start humming
an ancient fugue some hobo wrote.
There isn't anything gone wrong
that can't be fixed by railroad song.

A Frost Too Early

It's cruel October and the crow
is stripping bark from off the trees,
corn stalks shrivel, fall, and freeze.
Death hasn't any place to go
as shadows make a longer throw.
So up the hills and down the leas
he takes it as his right to seize
what life he left a spring ago.

And now the final apple falls,
the last red leaf lies curled.
The heart's machinery sputters, stalls.
What happened to the world?
At the door a knock comes steady.
Be gone. I'll tell you when I'm ready.

Adam's Other Rib

Life's a whisper, not a shout—
not even that without cats about.
Puss in boots, puss in trousers,
long, slick felines; fat, black mousers.
A cat who by his presence
speaks more than merely words.
Cats who bring home presents,
like half-dead mice and birds.

Cats in kitchens strolling
under sunlight preening, rolling.
Cats on little office trips
making tracks on manuscripts.
A dog's a dog, that's about that—
but only God can make a cat.

Airborne

Now as kites fly overhead
on ends of children spooling thread,
bells in temples start to chime.
Once for the living, twice for the dead,
thrice for the ones long gone ahead.
Four more tolls for the tick of time.
Five at least for the sake of rhyme
and six for the signs unread.

Bells give voice to the kites on high
that decorate otherwise empty sky.
Seven bells for the days of the week.
Eight for the mild, nine for the meek.
Ten bells apiece for you and me
and at least one more for the kite in the tree.

Ginger

All sausage curls and flying feet
she glides into the room.
She's going where the gauchos meet
and crowds shout *chick-a-boom.*
As rhythm rides the air, *con brio,*
she turns toward the chorus.
Come on, we're flying down to Rio.
I'll bet Brazilians will adore us.

Oh, lady of the silver screen
perched upon a stair,
you may not be quite what you seem
but I don't really care.
I love you in the swimming pool, ballroom or
    veranda,
I could not love you less were you Cavallero or
    Miranda.

Words Worth

Starting on the unlined page
we move toward its other end
not knowing if we'll meet the friend
we thought we might with age.
Words are little wars we wage,
paragraphs of let's pretend.
A period for proper end
will put the story in its cage.

But when the word is lost or gone
or stays away or doesn't come,
then Hell's the hand that moves the pen
in sonnet, signature, or song.
I don't know how it is for some;
for me it's endings without end.

The Scarlet Letter

So this is the way the world ends,
not with drops of Acid but buckets of Acid rain,
all the Anti-Additives A's decree, design, deign.
Anorexia, Alcohol, AIDS—it all depends
which A attacks the body until it screams Amen.
Apartheid sans Alternatives, White Africa's insane.
Addictions eat our Attitudes, Alzheimer's eats our
    brain.
But what's a few more Anxieties, amid a few less
    friends?

Youth dies early, Age endures.
Bring back Ailments Aspirin cures.
Those Anti-socials on the loose
have turned self-cult to self-Abuse.
As for the Awful letter A,
save the Alphabet, send it away.

Morning's
Diamond
Chambers

Mornings Enough

I cannot get enough
       of lit-up mornings,
birds shaking mist from low tree branches,
the early sky now shaved by clouds.
The hedgehog grumbling
          back to darkness
is known by me and loved by me.

Then settling in and moving fast,
mid-morning turns the cats to clowns
as round they spin
          in the butterfly chase,
tails twitching above the reeds.
Gotcha! No, the quarry's gone.
Cats lose interest long before noon,
even when low birds dive and tease.

Two to four in all its splendor
          renders description worthless.
The mirth of the moment
          moves to laughter
after the bell sounds five.
All, in a hurry, are off to the sunset
that trims the edge of house and hill.

Night is part of necessity's reach
for something a little more gentle.
Sentiment swings both low and high
and makes its practitioner
                    act without question,
to question his actions later.
The greater the darkness
                    the harder the loss,
and music costs more with the passing hour.

Ah, but consider
the lit-up mornings
when life does its sorting,
                    makes its decisions,
never too many, ever too few.

Hedgehogs with heads in daybooks,
grumbling, shuffling, jotting down
the start of the sunrise,
                    the debut of dawn.
I envy the sunlight wasting, wasted.
I mourn the mornings gone.

The Yellow Unicorn

This morning I woke up just in time to see
                              a yellow unicorn
eating the low branches from the linden tree outside—
then into the green he ran
and was gone.

Alone now—again
with sunlight the color of the unicorn
moving over the wall
                              and low clouds
and the hot July of New York about me,
I think about Diamante's green eyes,
or maybe the one called Dov
or others . . .

(I cannot forget
the images of some lone persons
who look at me and maybe for a while
                              seem to want me;
they wear love in their eyes
the way a child wears new
on his first day at school.)

I have loved some
whose arms and names I never knew,
the girl in Peter's bar,
                    a face on the train;
mostly in the last year
I've felt this kind of love.

And one night
hearing a big woman say
            as she was stroking my head
I wish there had been someone like you when I was
    young.
                    I went away
and began to love strangers,
people I would see only once
on buses and in bars or walking by themselves
                        in quiet places.
And in this last year there must have been a hundred
who never knew
a funny little boy watched *them* and loved
                                    them.

State Beach

He turned
and moved to go into the water;
she followed close behind.
The sun caught the color of her hair
and the bronze of his legs
and I caught them both,
held them in my gaze
till they were out of sight,
splashing in the sun,
lost in the waves.

I think I have never been in love more than now
here on a native beach,
watching other lovers
do familiar things and make familiar love.
I think I have never missed you more.

And as the last October sun
goes beyond the ocean to its resting place
and the umbrellas are folded,
the rumpled pants and rumpled dresses
slipped over the wet bathing suits,
the sound of Tokyo spring
echoes in my ears.
I walk with you down dark streets
and the rain comes down like tears.

Advice to the Second-Born

Marry someone with strong ripe hands,
the kind of man no fire intimidates.
The sort of a person who,
when told of your troubles, hums a tune,
presenting your troubles back to you.

Marry a man already tanned
so you will never have to be
                                    Sol's competition.
And there are hours and hours you'll save
by making the bedroom your only beach.

Marry a man well after the hunt
but well before he's "settled in."
If you would change him, coach him early.
Surprises are less welcome
after the preacher's been paid and gone.

Marry a man who'll give you children;
            don't let it go the other way.
A gift accepted has no strings.
The mistress then will be the master
over her brood and home.

If you expect to see him often,
marry a man whose gift is adequate.
With *genius* a roadshow always ongoing,
nothing can soften the time away
when nothing is all there is.

Marry a man unlike your father,
different in almost every way—
and you will always have a haven
when, stating some unacceptable reason,
the man you married turns to go.

Channing Way, 1

It's always the strangers that do the most damage,
the ones you never get to know,
                    seen in passing cars,
                              mirrored in windows
and remembered.
                    And the others—
the ones who promise everything, then go away.

Sometimes I think people were meant to be strangers,
not to get to know one another,
not to get close enough to damage the heart
made older by each new encounter.

But then,
someone comes along
and changes all that.
For a while anyway.

Still, as the years go by,
it's easier to remember
the streets where it happened
                    than the names
and who was the one on Channing Way?

Holidays

Holidays were made for lonely people.
I always meet the best of these
when holidays are near.
Rented rooms become the place to go,
                              not fireworks
or carnivals
              or musical parades,
but rented rooms with granite basins
and people who forget your name
before you finish going down the stairs.

Holidays mean the most
when you're celebrating
what you've found yourself.

Love is a season,
and holidays, like signposts,
mark the time.

I should have told you
that love is more
    than being warm in bed.
                      More
than individuals seeking an accomplice.
Even more than wanting to share.

I could have said
that love at best is giving what you need to get.

But it was raining
and we had no place to go,
and riding through the streets in a cab
                      I remembered
that words are only necessary after love has gone.

Day Song/Night Song

1.
The freckled morning
            moving into day now,
I stand at the window half dressed,
watching the snow melt as quickly as it falls.

A hundred blank windows
in the building now going up across the street
look back at me.
My expression is as empty as theirs,
as the long slow business
of learning how to live alone begins again.

2.
The shadowed afternoon
crawls away, becoming night.
I close the door behind me
and hurry down the stairs.

You know
Saturday night is better than Friday.
If you don't make out
you can take home
the great American consolation prize,
thirty cents' worth of love,
           the Sunday paper.

Morning Collection

In the half-light
we saw the swimmers
coming from the darkness
carrying the boy's body low,
as though its weight
was bending all of them
into the same submission,
as though the boy
was pulling them down too
the way the sea had pulled him
      to herself.

He was of course
just one more lover
of the gray-blue water,
a muscled boy who swam
a few yards farther out
              each day.
            But so young.
I wonder what he said
as he went down
that final time,
here I am or *let me go?*

I know the sea eats up
the men who love her most,
the way the killer queen
must finally one day
            reject the troops
who fought for her on battlefields
and fought with her in bedrooms.

I am not afraid.
I'd go down gladly in a whirlpool
if I had ridden all day
            on a friendly wave.

But one so young,
colorless, not even gasping,
too dead for even lonely.
A conscience cannot even wonder
            why.

For the sea
it was a little murder
done with might and yet no malice.
But what a poor repayment
for a man whose only crime
was to love the wild blue water
that in a single swallow
            tore and took him.

The sea gives up the living
as it does the recent dead;
at will it casts off what it will.

The ocean has a lesson
for our own lives
and those we take responsibility
                        toward.
Push forward, it keeps saying,
till your life is bare upon the shore,
until you're naked to yourself
                        and God.
The Christian and the Christless
are often gathered up and broken
on the same unflinching rock.

To wade the water is to learn.

You'll gain a guideline,
a watermark just like the sea,
that tells you how far you can travel
and still come home in certainty
             and safety.

Morning people
tracking down the shore
retrieve the best
and see the very worst
the sea sheds on the beach.

Hold on to me
and I'll become your enemy;
let me go and I'm your friend.
The ocean says that every day
a thousand and a thousand times.
And every evening,
her words having pounded
in our heads all day,
we repeat them
to each other
             as our own.

Wood Smoke

The geese above the pond
already call out winter
and wood smoke comes
from all the houses
in the town.

We'll move together then
and share the year's last warmness,
swallowing the rain like brandy.

The Distance to Monterey

Silence is a better means
for telegraphing thought
than any Morse code yet made.
I wonder if you know
how many conversations
we have had so far
with no words passed?
I often think our silence
has energy to get us
all the way to Monterey and back.

Time Enough

Find me friendly beasts
and I'll lie down
between their legs
easy and with ease.

Show me quiet shores
and I'll run down them
endlessly and without end
till my feet have blisters
from the polished sand.

Give me time enough
and I'll unwind, unset
all the clocks and watches
in the worldly world
so that I'll have time enough
to hike down quiet shores
with friendly beasts again.

Atlas

Don't be afraid
to fall asleep with gypsies
            or run with leopards.
As travelers or highwaymen
we should employ
whatever kind of wheels it takes
to make our lives
go smoothly down the road.

And if you love somebody,
            tell them.
Love's a better roadmap
for trucking down the years
than Rand McNally ever made.

For His Pleasure

Morning is the greatest architect,
the builder of the grass and clouds,
the maker of the anthems
            made for love and death,
the one whose testimony
will be passed from pasture up to hill,
and further up to hill above
by all things living,
            moving through its eyes.

The terrible detonations of the rain,
the bickering of the thunder
            from the sea,
the confidences betrayed by breeze
            and finally wind
cannot, together or alone,
affect the master draftsman, Morning.

The soul is blackened by the night.
Caught in its pitch with no road out,
the heart, the mind will stutter
                    and grow cold,
a little older and apart.
But nearly everything that's killed by dark
can be resurrected by the dawn,
that sweet designer of the river's thaw—
                    the ocean's rise and fall.

Morning is the greatest dreamer
                    of them all.
He is the first apostle of the living God,
the only one allowed to talk to trees
                    and hear the answers.

In the morning's diamond chambers
the daffodil is not forgotten.
The new-plowed field is damp, delicious,
and stretches, lifts toward eternity.

The sun now rising
comes to bake the ladybug's enamel
and with its wand ignites the grass, the leaf,
the aspirations of the dormant hedge.
Only in the A.M. hour
do these fires start the root to rise.
Between the two immensities of dusk and dawn
                lie only waiting hours,
time to waste or roundabout.

And man,
the littlest of all things
the first hour touches or makes up,
can only sigh as sunlight reaches him—
each sigh a little loss of life,
each bit of sunlight something
                        that regenerates the loss.
Morning, with its catalogue of hope,
has never seen the face of doubt,
not crippled poverty or crushing wealth,
only that creation and procreation
                        of itself.

Some naked piece of something
                    called Authority
will always try to take our Mornings
                    from us;
but we, its children, will resist, fight back,
                    until the Resurrection.
As the stars will not be harvested,
the subjects of the sun will not be bound.

Morning,
not the clang of hammers
                    or the clink of chain,
is the true reality—
the friend, the life, the romance
                    we know best.

HEART ATTACK

Getting Back to Us

Boundaries

I love you enough
to let you run
but far too much
to let you fly.

I'll let you walk
the block's end
          by yourself,
sail off on any lake
          or silent sea,
but if I peer at you
as you go wandering,
know that I keep watch
for both of us.

I love you enough
to let you run
but far too much
to let you fly.

An Evening Poem

I suppose that love is mindless.
Give it direction and off it goes.
Provide it with purpose and lose it.
Excuse it for being only love
          and expect a confrontation.
Remind it of its duties
and it will stay in bed asleep.

But let's pretend it's not unbalanced,
just for the sake of pretending.
Suppose it's a rose forever opening,
a wise little child that won't grow old.
How do you keep its center
                    from darkening?
Always lean it toward the light.
Give it the afternoon off when you can
but never a rest in the middle night.

In Case You Didn't Know

Some days up ahead
will come down empty
and some years fuller
than the fullest one
we've known before.

Today has been
the best day yet.

I thought
you ought
to know that,
and I thought it time
that I said *thank you*
for whatever might have
passed between us,
that in your mind
you might have felt
missed my attention.

It didn't
and it doesn't
and it won't.

Revision

Not content
to fly to Cedar Falls,
I'd like to track
the footprints on the moon
and carry home to you
a bouquet of space junk.

Because there is so little mystery
left in moonlight through the window
I'd like to bring you
one great armload of discarded
                            pristine stuff.
Cracked lenses off some Hasselblad,
K ration wrappers from Velveeta cheese,
and for your dressing table,
some not yet rusty wrench
that cost the government—
                            that's us—
a half a million bucks.

Surprises that no earthbound
jumble sale can boast
is what I'd like to give you.

If my old wink is worn
              or wearing out
hang on till I come home
              from out beyond,
entreating you with rocks and bolts
from lunar landscape.

Not just Gordon Cooper's underwear
but time capsule snapshots
            of his wife and kids
for you to tack up with those cards
I've been sending, you've collected
from the other worlds we've trucked to.

That Livingstone, Columbus
                and Magellan team
left Frank Sinatra records
                strewn about.
They won't play
on your Compact Disc machine
but I suspect you'll find a niche
for forty-fives and thirty-threes
the same as you have found a place
for this old relic, me.

Brownstone

Birds and butterflies
dart
    down
        canyons
between tall buildings,
looking for a place to hide
as the sky above the city darkens
and the rain begins,
        timid at first—unsure,
then creeping onto window ledges
and foraging along the sidewalk.

They're tearing down the building across the street
and the old woman who sat cushion-high
behind the flower boxes
        is gone.
Even the children who played along the broken side-
   walk
        have disappeared
and their hopscotch lines are washed away.

Only the multicolored cat,
preening in the shop window,
is unconcerned
as night begins.

Vacant Lot

Coming through
the twice-cracked concrete
in the vacant lot next door,
a sprig, not quite a tree
but strong and growing stronger,
surviving where a house
                    could not survive.
The house was trucked away
                        last summer,
board by board and brick by brick.

I never knew the family living there
as I've not had communion
with most communes
                congregated on this street.
Anyway, a sprig,
                not quite a tree,
is more sociable than any family
save a family of grass.
Not as friendly
as a well-loved animal,
but equal to the task
of being loved
        and loving.

Old Houses, One

I love old houses
          for their smells,
their must and dust and mildew
and for what they've been
to people I will never know.

The character
of caulked-up cracks
means more to me
than plastered walls and pretty paper,
walls that play the neighbor's music
when the radio I love
          has gone to sleep.

The faces of the old
are like old houses;
every line's a highway
          from the past.

And so I love old houses
and the faces that sit rocking
on their sagging porches.

Old Houses, Two

Back along the road to Moscow
                  and beyond,
the dachas of one hundred years
        or more
have the character
of park bench people
feeding squirrels and pigeons
from paper bags and reticules.
Their lines have deepened
and will deepen more.

New coats of paint
will brighten them
and gloss on smiles,
but the master painter still
is the brush and box
        of weather
and time the only artist
willing to take time.

It's proven on the fronts
of houses old and getting older
and the faces of the elderly.
Not old, seasoned only.

Old faces
are the premier class.
Old houses closing in at second,
not necessarily in age
but in history,
undramatic but imposing.

Whistle me a tune,
I ask a man
of undetermined
            years.
He does so,
smiling afterward
as if no one
had thought to ask him
such a question
or put a like task
            to him
any time before.

I could drift along
the Canal Grande
perceiving dwelling places
sinking slowly
and not feel sad.
Old houses earn
the right to die,
to crumble
and be gone
with no tears shed.

Furrows

Often I feel
the furrows on your forehead
are deep enough
to make a proper trench—
     and then you grin.

And I can see
blue sky again,
not just remember
when it was
that frost was absent
or on holiday.

Show me the rain,
you told me once,
then it rained every day.
Stop it, you said
     and I unable
crawled to my corner
and crouched there till
some brighter smile
     released me
by taking you away.

Grown up now,
youth given away,
reluctant to give up games.
What are the names
we go by:
Monopoly, me—
High Finance, you—
with hardly a Clue between us.

Another Monday, Two Months Later

Now I have the time
to take you riding
        in the car
to lie with you in private deserts
or eat with you
        in public restaurants.

Now I have the time
for football all fall long
and to apologize
for little lies and big lies
told when there was no time
to explain the truth.

I am finished
with whatever tasks
kept me from walking
in the woods with you
or leaping in the sand.

I have so much time
that I can build for you
sand castles out of mortar.

Mid-week picnics.
Minding my temper in traffic.
Washing your back
and cleaning out my closets.
Staying in bed with you
long past the rush hour
and the pangs of hunger.
    And listening
to the story of your life
in deadly detail.

Whatever time it takes,
I have the time.

I've have always wanted
to watch flowers open
all the way,
however long the process took.

I'd hoped that I might
take you traveling
down the block
or to wherever.

Now I have the time
to be bored,
to be delivered,
to be patient,
to be understanding,
to give you
all the time you need.

Now I have the time.
Where are you?

Words Above the Signature

Because the bulls run
one week out of fifty-two
down Pamplona side-streets
and I cannot outpace them
                    anymore.
And democracy's brass trumpets
blare from Spanish hill
            to Spanish hill
(all sound, even echo, fading
before the tune is put in practice),
and Mijas has a four-lane highway
                    to and from;
and just a ferry ride away,
a certain city in North Africa
sits poised to snap the tourist
                into a poppy snare.
I walk on tiptoes through
the red/pink/amber fields
that fan out from it,
if I walk fields at all.

Because the arson match is struck
even on God's vaulted ceiling
(never mind whole neighborhoods
now torched to cinder and all gone),
and fire forgets its subjects' names,
          is blind to street addresses—
confetti ashes spread across my yard,
one hundred miles from blazing brush.
Low animals that creep the ground
                    on fours,
are cooked to bones.

The lesser works of Big Magician
children, weak from circumstance,
powered men who battle flame
with fist and nozzle well connected
made poor and puny by a heat that seeks
and seizes all within its blanket reach.
A mother huddled in a bathtub,
lovers propagating on a Baldwin afternoon
                    no match for match.
I bury strikers deep.

Because the arsenals in every land
are piled and pyramiding out of sight—
thus out of conscientious mind;
men want the stepping stones to heaven
to be an alleyway of atoms
and there is no reversal anymore,
no rehearsal, just performance—
planned, unplanned, mistake,

                    unhappy accident—
a world that went
          before a second coming.

Because no drums are drumming out
                              BEWARE
and no strong voice from government
or pulpit cries out loud enough, *I care,*
I no longer look across my shoulder,
              worry over dented fenders
or try to figure out exactly why
some birds no longer sing the old songs.

Because this year
there might not be a Santa Claus,
I sign each letter I send out
        with love.
It is the shortest word I know for hope.

Because I have more reasons
                for *with love*
than paper I can put them on,
bill collector and computer generated page
will still get answers from me
with those words above my name.
It would not occur to me
to write *sincerely yours*
                or *best regards.*

Please don't think it's something personal
                (of course, it is).
I mean, *with love* is no big thing
except to sender and receiver.

You and me the true believers.

SLEEVE ON A HEART

Index of First Lines

About the Author

Rod McKuen was born in Oakland, California, in 1933. At eleven, he left home to work at jobs that took him throughout the western United States as rodman on a surveying unit, cowhand, lumberjack, ditchdigger, railroad worker, and finally rodeo cowboy. His first attention as a poet came in the early fifties, when he read with Kerouac and Ginsberg at San Francisco's Jazz Cellar. After serving two years as an infantryman in Korea, he returned as a singer of folksongs at San Francisco's Purple Onion. Before becoming a best-selling author in the 1960s, McKuen had been a contract player at Universal Studios and a vocalist with Lionel Hampton's band and had amassed a considerable following as a recording artist and nightclub performer.

His books, numbering more than forty titles, have been translated into some thirty languages and make him the best-selling, most widely read poet of his time. His film music has twice been nominated for Academy Awards (*The Prime of Miss Jean Brodie* and *A Boy Named Charlie Brown*). His classical works—symphonies, concertos, suites, and song cycles—are performed by leading orchestras and artists throughout the world. *The City: A Suite for Narrator & Orchestra*, commissioned by the Louisville Orchestra, was nominated for the Pulitzer Prize in Music.

He has written songs for nearly every important performer in the music business, producing standards that include "Love's Been Good to Me," "Jean," "I Think of You,"

"The World I Used to Know," "Rock Gently," and "I'll Catch the Sun." A nearly seventeen-year collaboration with Jacques Brel that McKuen terms equal parts of translation, adaptation, and collaboration produced "Seasons in the Sun," "If You Go Away," "The Port of Amsterdam," "The Far West," "I'm Not Afraid," and two dozen other songs. Those compositions, among others, have earned the writer-composer-performer more than forty gold and platinum records worldwide.

Rod McKuen poetry is currently taught in schools, colleges, universities, and seminaries around the world. He is recipient of the Carl Sandburg and Walt Whitman Awards for outstanding achievement in poetry and the Brandeis University Literary Trust Award for "continuing excellence and contributions to contemporary poetry."

In addition to his poetry, the author writes for United Features Syndicate and is a contributing editor and reviewer for various audio/video magazines including *Digital Audio, Video Review,* and *Stereo Review.* Throughout his life, McKuen has been a record and music collector, and is considered by many to have one of the world's largest private record collections.

HEART OF MY HEART

811.54 McKuen, Rod.
MCK
        Valentines

DISCARD

DATE		